LEGACY OF
LOVE

A Collection of Caribbean and Southern
Recipes Accentuated by Treasured
Photos and Memories

By Millicent Moore Hill

Trilogy Christian Publishers
A Wholly Owned Subsidiary of Trinity Broadcasting Network
2442 Michelle Drive
Tustin, CA 92780

Cover design by: Cornerstone Creative Solutions

For information, address Trilogy Christian Publishing
Rights Department, 2442 Michelle Drive, Tustin, Ca 92780.
Trilogy Christian Publishing/ TBN and colophon are trademarks of Trinity Broadcasting Network.

For information about special discounts for bulk purchases, please contact Trilogy Christian Publishing.

Manufactured in the United States of America

10 9 8 7 6 5 4 3 2 1

Library of Congress Cataloging-in-Publication Data is available.

ISBN 978-1-63769-238-7 (Print Book)
ISBN 978-1-63769-239-4 (ebook)

DEDICATION

In loving memory of Mildred E. Moore, a woman
who provided a soft, beautiful place for her family.

To Francine Smith, without her amazing help,
we couldn't have completed these recipes.
Francine, we will never be able to tell you how much we
appreciate your tremendous help. You will be missed.

About Mama Hill

I was born in Nashville, Tennessee at Meharry hospital, where my father was an intern. My father was an immigrant from South America. My mother was a very intelligent and beautiful Southern belle who graduated from college and was skilled in home economics. She told me my father was in competition with another young man with red hair who was courting her. The contest winner would be whoever could sit beside her the longest on the front porch. The poor guy could not out-sit Daddy, and he won her heart that day.

When I was born, my father was told that I wouldn't live past two days. I had rheumatic fever, pneumonia, and an enlarged heart. To this news, my father replied adamantly, "Oh, no—she's going to live! She has something to do!" That being said, he and my mother immediately held hands around me in a vigil of prayer. I'm told they did not leave beside my crib for at least three days as more people stepped in to check on me and pray. Though I was still very frail, they stayed and prayed over me until the crisis was over and I was out of danger. They placed little mittens on my hands because I would constantly scratch my face. Everyone labeled it a miracle that I had survived and lived despite the odds, and, as it turned out, I certainly did have a lot to do later in my life. Daddy was right.

About My Mother

My mother was a very efficient, loving person—very ladylike, delicate, and industrious. She actually taught me all of my organizational skills. She was a civil rights activist and a stay-at-home mom. I often watched her cook, and my brother and I both helped to make the sandwiches to go in our lunch boxes. One of my greatest memories was that we ate at the table together for dinner and engaged in open, intelligent conversations. We were given a voice in our household to speak our minds and express ourselves. My favorite dish was lamb roast with Worcestershire sauce on it.

Ladies and gentlemen, I hope you will share what I call "love food" and enjoy the spirit of love and life that should come from it.

Fried Chicken

What you'll need:
4 lbs. or more of chicken wings, or cut up 1 whole chicken
1-2 bags of Dixie Fry coating mix
1 tsp of smoked paprika
½ tsp of cayenne pepper
Peanut oil (or oil of choice)

Overnight marinade:
½ onion, grated
5 whole cloves of garlic, grated or crushed
½ cup of lemon juice
½ tsp salt

Optional additions to marinate:
Spicy mustard
Lemon pepper
Black or white pepper
Mrs. Dash original seasoning
Trader Joe's 21 Seasoning Salute

Steps:
1. Wash chicken first and refrigerate until ready to season.
2. Place washed chicken pieces in the marinade. Cover it and marinate overnight.
3. When ready to prepare, add optional seasonings to marinated chicken. See above.

4. Use 1 to 2 bags of Dixie Fry coating.
5. Shake chicken so that excess marinade falls off of it.
6. Place chicken in the bag of flour coating.
7. Shake flour and seasoned chicken thoroughly.
8. Use the peanut oil or oil of your choice to fry chicken (if you're going to deep fry it, you'll need to have a full container of oil, and the deep skillets are very nice).
9. Heat the oil and lower chicken one by one into the deep hot oil.
10. Let it fry for 4 to 10 minutes to capture the moisture.
11. Uncover the chicken, and let it fry for another 5 to 10 minutes. Do not fry for more than 20 to 30 minutes in hot oil. Lower heat if the flour gets too dark.

Salmon Pie

What you'll need:
2 frozen pie shells
2 cans of pink salmon (remove bones)
½ tbsp of lemon pepper
½ tbsp of garlic powder
½ tbsp of onion powder
½ cup of chopped onions
½ cup of chopped bell peppers
1 tsp of oregano
1 egg
Oil of your choice

Steps:
1. Sauté the salmon, onions, and bell peppers in the oil of your choice.
2. Mix all seasoning ingredients to create the salmon mix: lemon pepper, garlic powder, onion powder, and oregano.
3. Beat one egg and add it to the seasoning mix.
4. Add the sauteed salmon and onions to the mix.
5. Spread the salmon mix into the pie shells.
6. Bake pies for approximately 15 to 20 minutes.
7. Watch them until the crust is done. You'll know when the salmon is cooked because the egg will be firm.

A Crabmeat Casserole Holiday Story

Christopher Moore—Grandson

As a child, you can always tell when it's going to be a special occasion. The house is cleaned from top to bottom. The steamed water goblets come out. The dining room table is extended by placing the large board in the middle to provide more seating. This only happened on special dates. The regular turkey dressing and traditional holiday meal were prepared with an added treat for special occasions. This treat was my grandmother's special crabmeat casserole. It was special because crabmeat was expensive, but it took careful time putting together the cheese, heavy cream, milk, noodles, and of course, the topping of baked bread. The crumbs were browned to perfection with real butter and chopped onions. It was not only beautiful to look at, but rich and delicious. My grandmother's casserole was always the talk of the holiday table.

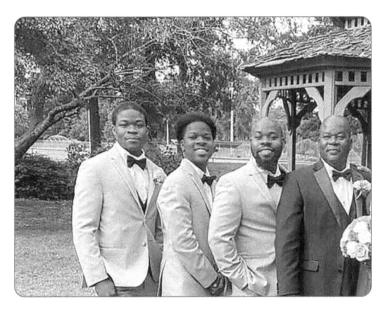

Crab Casserole

What you'll need:
Shredded crab or imitation crab
½ stick of butter
1 tbsp of black pepper
1 tbsp of lemon pepper
½ or 1 cup of milk or substitute for milk
½ cup of lemon juice
1 bag of egg noodles
1 ½ tbsp of flour (for white cream sauce)
Small amount of Worcestershire sauce
1 cup of shredded jack cheese

Optional:
Garlic powder .
Onion powder

Steps:
1. In a skillet, add flour in butter until the flour is slightly browned and thick.
2. Add a small amount of lemon juice.
3. Add a small amount of Worcestershire sauce and milk. Continue stirring.
4. Add in the rest of seasoning to create the cream sauce.
5. Boil noodles in another pot.
6. In a casserole dish, place a layer of boiled noodles. Then, add a layer of shredded crab meat.

7. Add shredded jack cheese on top of that and then another layer of noodles.
8. Pour cream sauce or white sauce on top of that layer.
9. Repeat the layering until you're at the top. Add cheese on top.
10. Place the casserole in a preheated oven for approximately 30 minutes until ready.

Crab and Lobster Casserole

What you'll need:
1 package of egg noodles
2 lbs. of lobster and crab meat
Breadcrumbs
White sauce (see crab casserole recipe)

Steps:
1. Prepare white sauce using the same ingredients from the crab casserole.
2. In a skillet, add the flour and butter until it starts to thicken. Continue stirring.
3. Add ½ cup of lemon juice and 1 tbsp of Worcestershire sauce.
4. Use a Pyrex dish or a baking dish (square or rectangular) to layer the casserole.
5. Begin with a layer of noodles, then crab and lobster, then pour the cream sauce over it. Repeat.
6. You may also use shredded cheddar cheese or ricotta cheese for richness.
7. Add breadcrumbs at the very top.
8. Bake for approximately 25 minutes.

Here's a list of low-sodium seasonings as substitutions:
- 21 Seasoning Salute (Trader Joe's)
- Mrs. Dash
- Sea Salt/Himalayan Salt
- Cilantro

- Unsalted garlic powder
- Unsalted onion powder

Lower cholesterol oils:
- Olive oil
- Grapeseed oil
- Peanut oil

Meatloaf

What you'll need:
3 lbs. ground turkey or chicken or beef
1 to 1 ½ onion, chopped
1 to 1 ½ bell pepper, chopped
1 tsp of garlic powder
1 tsp of onion powder
1 tsp of Worcestershire sauce
1 egg
½ cup to 1 cup of breadcrumbs
1 tbsp of lemon pepper
Pinch of sugar (optional)
½ pack of taco seasoning (optional)

Glaze:
½ cup of brown sugar
½ cup of tomato ketchup
1 tbsp of Worcestershire sauce
1 tbsp of spicy mustard or ground mustard

Steps:
1. Using your hands, mix the ground meat with all seasoning ingredients. Add breadcrumbs, chopped onions and peppers, Worcestershire sauce, and egg.
2. Once thoroughly mixed, mold the ground meat into a nice shape.

3. As an option, you can put two boiled eggs right in the center of the ground meat so when you cut the meat, the egg will show. It's a nice, tasty surprise.
4. Prepare the glaze mixture.
5. When the meatloaf is done cooking in the oven, take it out and spread the glaze on top. Then, place it back in the oven for 10 to 15 minutes.

Chicken and Dumplings

What you'll need:
4 lbs. of chicken
1 box or 2 cans of chicken broth
1 tbsp of garlic powder
1 tbsp of onion powder
1 tsp of lemon pepper
½ cup of chopped onions
Pepper flakes (to taste)
Flour tortillas ("dumplings") cut into strips
1 can of cream of mushroom

Steps:
1. Make a marinade with all the seasoning ingredients and rub it all over the chicken.
2. Cook the chicken on the stove or in a crock pot until tender. Shred the chicken into pieces.
3. Take flour tortillas and cut them into strips.
4. Add them to the mixture.
5. Add cream of mushroom soup to taste.
6. You can also add extra veggies like English peas, corn, or okra.

Easter Sunday Leg of Lamb Roast

*This recipe may also be used for pork or beef roast.

What you'll need:
1 whole lamb roast
5 sprigs of rosemary
1 can of chicken or beef broth
8 cloves of garlic
1 tbsp of onion powder
1 tbsp of black pepper
1 tbsp of white pepper
1 tbsp of lemon pepper
1 tbsp of spicy mustard (optional)

Steps:
1. Create a dry rub for the lamb using all the seasoning.
2. Poke holes with a knife in the lamb roast.
3. Stick large whole cloves of garlic in each of the slots.
4. Now, rub the seasoning all over and into the lamb. You can also use spicy mustard of any type over the lamb if you want.
5. Let it sit in the fridge overnight or up to 2 days covered with foil. The longer it marinates, the better.
6. Bake at a very low temperature until nice and tender.

Cabbage

What you'll need:
1 head of cabbage, chopped or shredded
1 chopped onion
1 chopped bell pepper
1 tbsp of your favorite barbecue sauce

Steps:
1. Rinse cabbage and set aside.
2. Sauté the onion and bell pepper in grapeseed oil or olive oil.
3. Add cabbage, salt, and pepper and let it steam to your satisfaction, whether crisp or very soft.
4. Add a tablespoon of barbecue sauce for a smoky flavor.
5. Let it continue to steam until ready to serve.

Green Beans

*Same recipe as the previous cabbage dish, but without the bell pepper.

What You'll Need:
2 cans of green beans
Ingredients listed for cabbage recipe (except bell pepper)

Steps:
1. The cabbage recipe can be used for green beans, although I do not suggest the bell pepper.
2. Sauté the onions.
3. Add a tablespoon of barbecue sauce and onions to the green beans.
4. Cook for 10 to 15 minutes.

Salmon Steak

What you'll need:
1 to 2 salmon fillets
1 tbsp of Mrs. Dash seasoning
½ onion, chopped
1 bell pepper, chopped
1 tbsp of lemon juice

Steps:
1. Season the salmon with your seasoning rub (and lemon juice).
2. Sauté the onions and bell pepper.
3. Place the sauteed onion mix on top of the salmon fillets.
4. Place the salmon on a skillet and bake until done for approximately 20 to 25 minutes. Keep checking on it so it does not overcook.
5. Once cooked, you can sprinkle some dill on top of the salmon.

Salmon and Rice Dish

What you'll need:
1 can of salmon
1 can of tomato sauce
2 cups of cooked white rice
½ onion chopped
1 bell pepper, chopped

Steps:
1. Saute the onion and bell pepper with your oil of choice.
2. Add tomato sauce to the sauteed mix.
3. Once cooked down, you can season it with salt and pepper to taste, and then pour it over your rice to serve!
4. You can also use the same recipe to make a tasty omelet.

Thanksgiving Turkey

Steps:
1. Rub your turkey with the seasoning you like.
2. Take a large piece of gauze. Soak it in butter until it's fully saturated.
3. Place it over the turkey and roast it until it's completely done.

Turkey, Gizzards, & Liver

What you'll need:
Poultry seasoning
1 tsp of salt
½ cup of celery
½ cup of onions
Turkey giblets (cut into small pieces)
1 can of chicken broth (or juice from the cooked turkey)
Pepper and seasoning to taste

Steps:
1. Boil the giblets (after cutting them up into small pieces) with sauteed onion and celery.
2. Add the seasoning and broth.
3. Add this mixture to your dressing recipe and bake it. You can also use it as a gravy if you don't want to add giblets to dressing.
4. You may also season the inside of the turkey and place vegetables inside.

Gravy

1.   Using the broth from the turkey or butter, sprinkle a tablespoon of flour into the hot butter or broth. Stir it and add broth until it is the right thick consistency.

Dressing

What you'll need:
Cornbread dressing
Poultry seasoning
1 tbsp of dried sage
1 cup of diced onions
1 can of turkey broth

Steps:
1.   Crunch up the dressing with all the seasoning ingredients.
2.   Pour the broth over the dressing and stir it all together.
3.   Spread the dressing mix in a baking dish.
4.   Bake it for 20 to 30 minutes and check it for progress.

Doctor Granddaddy:
Jeremiah Moore

My father was an immigrant from South America who worked his way to the United States on a banana boat. Upon arrival in New York, he became a teacher. Then, he moved to Nashville, Tennessee and enrolled into Fisk University, where he majored in pre-medicine. Finally, he graduated from Meharry Medical School as a general practitioner. His first practice was in Dyersburg, Tennessee, where he became the only African American country doctor in the county. He founded a youth center, and he was an advisor to many young people, including myself.

Both of my parents were heavily involved in the civil rights movement. In those days, African Americans were not allowed to be treated inside the hospital, which led my father to make many house calls. I remember one house call in particular where my father had to take the entire family on the call to protect us from the Ku Klux Klan. We arrived close to the patient's home where we had to stop and wait for a wagon drawn by two horses to complete the journey to the house due to the mud in our path that replaced the road. We arrived at the house, where he was to deliver a baby. It had one large room that contained a kitchen and bed where the birth was going to take place. We actually saw the baby delivered, the umbilical cord cut, the baby dressed in a white clean pillowcase with holes cut in it. Then, he placed the baby on a pillow in a dresser drawer. My father was paid with canned vegetables and a whole hog during slaughter time. Even though I was young, I was really awestruck by the miracle that I had just witnessed. My brother slept through the whole thing—he was just a toddler.

Approximately five years from that time, our family moved to Pasadena, California because of my poor health; this is where Dr. Jeremiah Moore became a very popular house call doctor, and also where he and my mother continued their political activism. By the time my brother and I were reaching college age, there was one unfortunate incident of drama that stopped my father's practice temporarily. It was devastating, but he continued to take very good care of his family and recover.

However, in 1964, my father became ill with brain cancer. Fortunately, he was able to meet my two children in the hospital. I remember on that morning before he passed, even though I was in Oklahoma City, I felt his presence at the foot of my bed as I slept. I could sense in my spirit he was gone. The phone rang abruptly as it woke me out of my sleep before my brother could say anything. I quickly asked, "Daddy's gone, isn't he?" He replied, "Yes," in a trembling voice. At his funeral, I wrote and read a poem where I promised to carry on his work in the world. I have, and so it is!

James Baldwin party hosts and hostesses

Early Childhood here "Fun Fun Furn"

Precious Memories

I remember when my mother discovered that she had cancer. She prayed that she would live to see her children grow up and have children of their own. She did just that!

I remember when she became a civil rights worker and worked with parents in the community for the rights of those who were less fortunate.

I remember when James Baldwin came to our house and sat in our big weeping willow tree on the patio and spoke to the people of the community. My friends and I were told to dress up so we could play hosts and hostesses for that event.

I remember when my brother and I had our first party. My mother made her famous punch, and we practiced dancing with the doorknob. We were so nervous because it was going to be our first party!

I remember when my mother let me wear my first pair of stockings with a pair of kitten shoes.

I remember when my parents went to San Francisco to renew their wedding vows and my father gave her the ring that I wear on my finger now.

I remember when we prayed together at dinner and had intellectual conversations around the table. My father sat at the head of the table and my mother at the other end. The family dinners always made me feel safe and loved. The lamb roast was one of my favorite dishes.

I remember when my mother did all the fancy decorations for Christmas. She made her fruitcakes, pies, and eggnog in advance and was so joyful.

I remember when my family received backlash for standing up in the community for obvious racism. My father took the brunt of it, but my mother stood right by him.

I remember when we made our bologna sandwiches for the week and would pack them in our lunchboxes for school.

I remember when my mother took care of my grandfather and bathed him when he became ill.

I remember my mother made all my dresses from Vogue patterns.

I remember when I was accepted to Fisk University, and the whole family flew back to Nashville with me. I almost had an anxiety attack, as it was the first time I was leaving home.

You are cordially invited
to have coffee with

Mr. James Baldwin
Essayist and Novelist

Saturday, May 11, 1963   9 to 11 a.m

at the home of
Dr. and Mrs. Jeremiah Moore
1157 Armada Drive, Pasadena, California

Sponsored by Pasadena CORE

Donation -

James Baldwin invitation

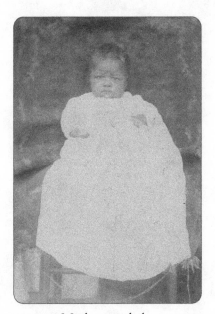

Mother as a baby

Girly-Girl Talk

Woman to Woman

One fine night long ago, my mom and I had a little tete-a-tete in the living room. She didn't really drink, but we each had a glass of red wine. As we were talking, one glass led to another, and for the first time, she and I really opened up to each other. She told me about her sadness and her anger with her mom because of a "me too" incident in which her mom was in total denial. She said that's why she always played the piano and sang "Come Ye Disconsolate." However, she said even though her mom was distant from her and sometimes angry with her, as she grew older, especially when she got married and had us, she realized that her mom could not really do any better because of her own pain. So, she made up her mind to have the best life she could possibly have, and she decided to create an environment that was beautiful for her husband and her two children. She threw away all the anger.

That was a relief for her to tell me that on her third glass of wine, and of course, I shared the sadness and disappointment of my divorce; the trauma of seeing something that broke my heart. However, I, too, had finally come to the conclusion that I was somebody, and I would love myself and be the best "somebody" that I could ever be! By this time, it was the fourth glass of wine, and for us—because we didn't drink—we were highly inebriated. So, what was the next thing to do? We fell into each other's arms and cried with joy because we had discovered our value, our love for each other, and our love for everyone else in our pathways. Oh, freedom! Oh, freedom! That's what that was.

Warm Goodbyes

The Final Call

It was a beautiful Sunday morning, and for some reason I was anxious to go visit my mom in Pasadena, but one thing after another happened. As I was driving, I got a flat tire on the freeway and had to pull over and call AAA. On top of that, the car wouldn't start. So, AAA had to go and get me another battery. All of these things happened, and I was frustrated. I just wanted to get to her.

It took half the afternoon, but finally I made it to her house and to her bedside. The caregiver told me that she was having a bad day. She really was, because she almost didn't remember me. So, I sat next to her on her bed, and she said, "Is that you, Millicent?" I said, "Yes. Would you like for me to read to you, Mommy? What would you like for me to do?" She said, "Yes. Read me the twenty-third Psalm."

I reached for the Bible at the head of the bed and started reading to her. She read with me, and we ended up reading it twice. That seemed to brighten her spirit. Then, she said, "Baby, can you oil my feet? I think it's time for that." That frightened me somewhat, because in our house, we only oiled the feet of the woman if she was having a child or when she was about to die. So, I paused for a moment. Then, I started rubbing her feet with the baby oil. She started singing "Come Ye Disconsolate," her favorite song, and I joined in with her. We sang all the verses. She seemed really calm.

When we finished, there was a long pause of silence. So, I took her hand, and I just crawled in the bed next to her. She said, "I'm tired now. I'm going to take a little nap. Are you going to stay with me a little while?" I said, "Yes, Mommy. I'm right here." She fell asleep holding my hand, and I dozed off for a few moments. The caregiver came in and said, "In a minute I'll have to get her ready for bed and fix her food." So, I got up and cleaned her room as best as I could. When I checked the time, I noticed it was time for me to get back on the freeway before it got too dark. She woke up for a moment and said, "You leaving me?" I said, "Yes." She said, "Will you be back next Sunday?" I said, "Of course, and I'll bring you some chocolates." I kissed her gently on the forehead and left, but with a strange feeling in my heart. Even as I was driving on the freeway, I had that empty feeling.

I had just made it in before dark. I got up the steps, out of my clothes, and sat in my chair. Just then, my brother called me, and he said, "We're on the way to the hospital. Mom passed out while she was eating." I said, "Should I drive back?" He said she'd be alright, so I sat back in my chair and began to pray for the peace that surpasses all understanding and for God's will to be done. Ten minutes later, he called me back, and I reluctantly picked up the phone. He said, "Mill, she's gone. We just barely got in the hospital door. She's gone." I just closed my eyes and held my head back. I'm so glad I spent that time with her. She knew her little feet had to be oiled. I just started singing her song again: "Come ye disconsolate. Where'er you languish. Come to the mercy seat. Fervently kneel. Earth has no sorrow that heaven cannot heal." A rush of joy filled my heart. I smiled as a tear fell from my eyes.

Come, Ye Disconsolate

Come, ye disconsolate, where'er ye languish;
Come to the mercy-seat, fervently kneel;
Here bring your wounded hearts, here tell your anguish,
Earth has no sorrow that heaven cannot heal.

Joy of the comfortless, light of the straying,
Hope of the penitent, fadeless and pure;
Here speaks the Comforter, tenderly saying—
Earth has no sorrow that heaven cannot cure.

Here see the Bread of Life; see waters flowing
Forth from the throne of God, pure from above;
Come to the feast of love; come, ever knowing
Earth has no sorrow but heaven can remove.

Mother's first boyfriend

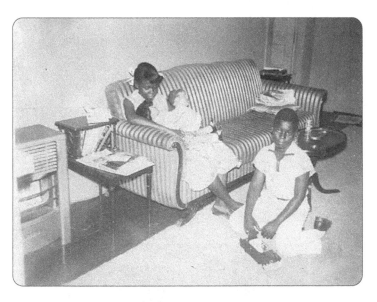